Animals' party

by Hilary Lazell

Illustrated by Angela Mills

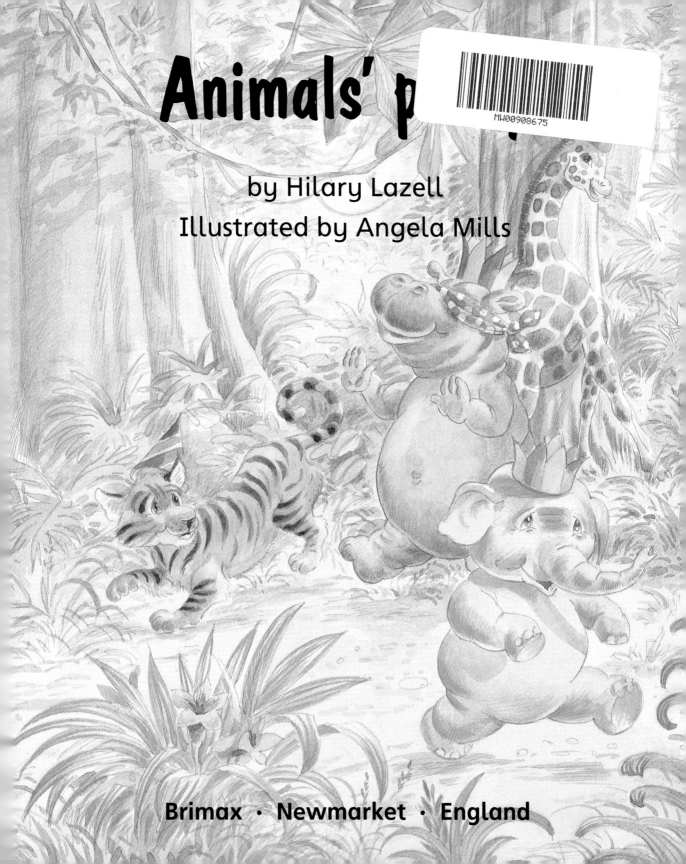

Brimax · Newmarket · England

Harry Hippo lives deep in the jungle. He is a very kind, friendly hippo but he is also the dirtiest, smelliest animal in the jungle. Whenever it is time to bathe in the lake, Harry runs the other way. His mother is in despair.

"I do not know what to do with Harry," she says to Mrs Giraffe. "I do not think he likes water." Harry does not like water. "It is too wet and cold," he moans as his mother tucks him up in bed.

"If you do not have a bath soon, no-one will play with you," warns his mother. "In fact, no-one will know who you are, you are covered in so much mud."
She holds her nose and kisses him goodnight. He really is far too smelly to be near.

There is one type of bath that Harry likes and that is a mud bath. When he is tired of playing with his friends or when they are tired of the smell, Harry goes to a mud hole and rolls over in the slimy mud until he is covered from head to foot. Needless to say, swarms of flies follow him home, but everyone else stays out of his way.

One day, Harry finds all his friends whispering excitedly. "Ssh. Here comes Harry," says Eric Elephant. All the animals run off.
"I wonder what all that is about," says Harry.

Later he finds his friends' mothers whispering together. "Ssh. Here comes Harry," says Mrs Tiger. They all rush off to get their children for their baths.

When Harry reaches home he tells his mother how strangely the other animals have been acting.

"I think they are planning a surprise," says Harry. "I love surprises." He is too tired to notice the worried look on his mother's face, and he falls asleep dreaming about what the surprise can be. The next day Harry meets some of his friends.

"Sorry we cannot play, we have to get ready for the party," they say. And they all run off.

So that is the surprise. But no-one has told Harry to get ready! Where is the party being held? Harry heads to his mud hole.

Just past the lake in the big clearing, hanging between two trees, is a 'WELCOME TO THE PARTY' banner. Harry cannot believe his eyes. There are hundreds of balloons and tables full of food. Just as he is near enough to smell the food, someone comes rushing up to him. It is Granny Elephant.

"Go away! Shoo! You nasty, smelly object! Do not go near the party food! Now be off with you!" And she chases poor Harry away from the clearing. Harry runs as fast as his legs will carry him, tears streaming down his face.

He has not been invited to the party. No-one wants him there. Harry flops down on the grass and sobs enormous wet tears. A long time and many tears later Harry stands up, shakes himself dry and wanders miserably on, not noticing in which direction he is going.

Before he realises it he is
back at the clearing where the
party is.

"Look! It is Harry!" cries
someone. "And he is clean!"
Everyone rushes over.

"Well done! You look quite
handsome," says Gerry Giraffe.
Harry looks at his reflection
in the lake. It is true, he
is clean! All his tears have
washed the dirt away!

Harry's mother comes up behind him. "I am proud of you, Harry," she whispers. Harry glows with happiness. Now that he is clean he can join the party. Later, as he tucks into his third bowl of cake and ice-cream, Harry promises that he will never go near a mud hole again. Well not for a few days, anyway!

Say these words again

friendly

really

swarms

strangely

surprise

chases

smelliest

covered

whispering

dreaming

between

handsome